Travel phrasebooks collection
«Everything Will Be Okay»
...blishing

PHRA EBOOK

— SERBIAN —

THE MOST IMPORTANT PHRASES

This phrasebook contains the most important phrases and questions for basic communication
Everything you need to survive overseas

By Andrey Taranov

T&P BOOKS

Phrasebook + 250-word dictionary

English-Serbian phrasebook & mini dictionary

By Andrey Taranov

The collection of "Everything Will Be Okay" travel phrasebooks published by T&P Books is designed for people traveling abroad for tourism and business. The phrasebooks contain what matters most - the essentials for basic communication. This is an indispensable set of phrases to "survive" while abroad.

You'll also find a mini dictionary with 250 useful words required for everyday communication - the names of months and days of the week, measurements, family members, and more.

T&P Books Publishing
www.tpbooks.com

ISBN: 978-1-78492-405-8

This book is also available in E-book formats.
Please visit www.tpbooks.com or the major online bookstores.

FOREWORD

The collection of "Everything Will Be Okay" travel phrasebooks published by T&P Books is designed for people traveling abroad for tourism and business. The phrasebooks contain what matters most - the essentials for basic communication. This is an indispensable set of phrases to "survive" while abroad.

This phrasebook will help you in most cases where you need to ask something, get directions, find out how much something costs, etc. It can also resolve difficult communication situations where gestures just won't help.

This book contains a lot of phrases that have been grouped according to the most relevant topics. You'll also find a mini dictionary with useful words - numbers, time, calendar, colors...

Take "Everything Will Be Okay" phrasebook with you on the road and you'll have an irreplaceable traveling companion who will help you find your way out of any situation and teach you to not fear speaking with foreigners.

TABLE OF CONTENTS

T&P Books Publishing

PRONUNCIATION

Letter	Serbian example	T&P phonetic alphabet	English example

Vowels

Letter	Serbian example	T&P phonetic alphabet	English example
А а	авлија	[a]	shorter than in ask
Е е	ексер	[e]	elm, medal
И и	излаз	[i]	shorter than in feet
О о	очи	[o]	pod, John
У у	ученик	[u]	book

Consonants

Letter	Serbian example	T&P phonetic alphabet	English example
Б б	брег	[b]	baby, book
В в	вода	[ʋ]	vase, winter
Г г	глава	[g]	game, gold
Д д	дим	[d]	day, doctor
Ђ ђ	ђак	[dʑ]	jeans, gene
Ж ж	жица	[ʒ]	forge, pleasure
З з	зец	[z]	zebra, please
Ј ј	мој	[j]	yes, New York
К к	киша	[k]	clock, kiss
Л л	лептир	[l]	lace, people
Љ љ	љиљан	[ʎ]	daily, million
М м	мајка	[m]	magic, milk
Н н	нос	[n]	name, normal
Њ њ	књига	[ɲ]	canyon, new
П п	праг	[p]	pencil, private
Р р	рука	[r]	rice, radio
С с	слово	[s]	city, boss
Т т	тело	[t]	tourist, trip
Ћ ћ	ћуран	[tɕ]	cheer
Ф ф	фењер	[f]	face, food
Х х	хлеб	[h]	home, have
Ц ц	цео	[ts]	cats, tsetse fly
Ч ч	чизме	[ʧ]	church, French

Letter	Serbian example	T&P phonetic alphabet	English example
Џ џ	џбун	[ʤ]	joke, general
Ш ш	шах	[ʃ]	machine, shark

LIST OF ABBREVIATIONS

English abbreviations

ab.	-	about
adj	-	adjective
adv	-	adverb
anim.	-	animate
as adj	-	attributive noun used as adjective
e.g.	-	for example
etc.	-	et cetera
fam.	-	familiar
fem.	-	feminine
form.	-	formal
inanim.	-	inanimate
masc.	-	masculine
math	-	mathematics
mil.	-	military
n	-	noun
pl	-	plural
pron.	-	pronoun
sb	-	somebody
sing.	-	singular
sth	-	something
v aux	-	auxiliary verb
vi	-	intransitive verb
vi, vt	-	intransitive, transitive verb
vt	-	transitive verb

Serbian abbreviations

ж	-	feminine noun
ж мн	-	feminine plural
м	-	masculine noun
м мн	-	masculine plural
мн	-	plural
с	-	neuter
с мн	-	neuter plural

SERBIAN
PHRASEBOOK

This section contains
important phrases that may
come in handy in various
real-life situations.
The phrasebook will help
you ask for directions, clarify
a price, buy tickets, and
order food at a restaurant

T&P Books Publishing

PHRASEBOOK
CONTENTS

T&P Books Publishing

The bare minimum

Excuse me, ...	**Извините, ...** Izvinite, ...
Hello.	**Добар дан.** Dobar dan
Thank you.	**Хвала вам.** Hvala vam
Good bye.	**Довиђења.** Doviđenja
Yes.	**Да.** Da
No.	**Не.** Ne
I don't know.	**Не знам.** Ne znam
Where? | Where to? | When?	**Где? | Куда? | Када?** Gde? | Kuda? | Kada?
I need ...	**Треба ми ...** Treba mi ...
I want ...	**Хоћу ...** Hoću ...
Do you have ...?	**Имате ли ...?** Imate li ...?
Is there a ... here?	**Да ли овде постоји ...?** Da li ovde postoji ...?
May I ...?	**Смем ли ...?** Smem li ...?
..., please (polite request)	**молим** molim
I'm looking for ...	**Тражим ...** Tražim ...
restroom	**тоалет** toalet
ATM	**банкомат** bankomat
pharmacy (drugstore)	**апотеку** apoteku
hospital	**болницу** bolnicu
police station	**полицијску станицу** policijsku stanicu
subway	**метро** metro

taxi	**такси** taksi
train station	**железничку станицу** železničku stanicu

My name is …	**Ја се зовем …** Ja se zovem …
What's your name?	**Како се ви зовете?** Kako se vi zovete?
Could you please help me?	**Да ли бисте, молим вас, могли да ми помогнете?** Da li biste, molim vas, mogli da mi pomognete?
I've got a problem.	**Имам проблем.** Imam problem
I don't feel well.	**Не осећам се добро.** Ne osećam se dobro
Call an ambulance!	**Позовите хитну помоћ!** Pozovite hitnu pomoć!
May I make a call?	**Смем ли да телефонирам?** Smem li da telefoniram?

I'm sorry.	**Извините …** Izvinite …
You're welcome.	**Нема на чему.** Nema na čemu

I, me	**ја, мене** ja, mene
you (inform.)	**ти** ti
he	**он** on
she	**она** ona
they (masc.)	**они** oni
they (fem.)	**оне** one
we	**ми** mi
you (pl)	**ви** vi
you (sg, form.)	**ви** vi

ENTRANCE	**УЛАЗ** ULAZ
EXIT	**ИЗЛАЗ** IZLAZ
OUT OF ORDER	**НЕ РАДИ** NE RADI

CLOSED	**ЗАТВОРЕНО** ZATVORENO
OPEN	**ОТВОРЕНО** OTVORENO
FOR WOMEN	**ЗА ЖЕНЕ** ZA ŽENE
FOR MEN	**ЗА МУШКАРЦЕ** ZA MUŠKARCE

Questions

Where?	**Где?** Gde?
Where to?	**Куда?** Kuda?
Where from?	**Одакле?** Odakle?
Why?	**Зашто?** Zašto?
For what reason?	**Из ког разлога?** Iz kog razloga?
When?	**Када?** Kada?
How long?	**Колико дуго?** Koliko dugo?
At what time?	**У колико сати?** U koliko sati?
How much?	**Колико?** Koliko?
Do you have ...?	**Имате ли ...?** Imate li ...?
Where is ...?	**Где се налази ...?** Gde se nalazi ...?
What time is it?	**Колико је сати?** Koliko je sati?
May I make a call?	**Смем ли да телефонирам?** Smem li da telefoniram?
Who's there?	**Ко је тамо?** Ko je tamo?
Can I smoke here?	**Да ли се овде пуши?** Da li se ovde puši?
May I ...?	**Смем ли ...?** Smem li ...?

Needs

I'd like …	**Волео /Волела/ бих …** Voleo /Volela/ bih …
I don't want …	**Не желим …** Ne želim …
I'm thirsty.	**Жедан /Жедна/ сам.** Žedan /Žedna/ sam
I want to sleep.	**Хоћу да спавам.** Hoću da spavam

I want …	**Хоћу …** Hoću …
to wash up	**да се освежим** da se osvežim
to brush my teeth	**да оперем зубе** da operem zube
to rest a while	**да се мало одморим** da se malo odmorim
to change my clothes	**да се пресвучем** da se presvučem

to go back to the hotel	**да се вратим у хотел** da se vratim u hotel
to buy …	**да купим …** da kupim …
to go to …	**да идем до …** da idem do …
to visit …	**да посетим …** da posetim …
to meet with …	**да се нађем са …** da se nađem sa …
to make a call	**да телефонирам** da telefoniram

I'm tired.	**Уморан /Уморна/ сам.** Umoran /Umorna/ sam
We are tired.	**Ми смо уморни.** Mi smo umorni
I'm cold.	**Хладно ми је.** Hladno mi je
I'm hot.	**Вруће ми је.** Vruće mi je
I'm OK.	**Добро сам.** Dobro sam

I need to make a call.

Треба да телефонирам.
Treba da telefoniram

I need to go to the restroom.

Морам до тоалета.
Moram do toaleta

I have to go.

Морам да идем.
Moram da idem

I have to go now.

Морам одмах да идем.
Moram odmah da idem

Asking for directions

Excuse me, ...	**Извините ...** Izvinite ...
Where is ...?	**Где се налази ...?** Gde se nalazi ...?
Which way is ...?	**Куда до ...?** Kuda do ...?
Could you help me, please?	**Можете ли ми, молим вас, помоћи?** Možete li mi, molim vas, pomoći?
I'm looking for ...	**Тражим ...** Tražim ...
I'm looking for the exit.	**Тражим излаз.** Tražim izlaz
I'm going to ...	**Идем до ...** Idem do ...
Am I going the right way to ...?	**Јесам ли на правом путу до ...?** Jesam li na pravom putu do ...?
Is it far?	**Да ли је далеко?** Da li je daleko?
Can I get there on foot?	**Могу ли до тамо пешке?** Mogu li do tamo peške?
Can you show me on the map?	**Можете ли да ми покажете на мапи?** Možete li da mi pokažete na mapi?
Show me where we are right now.	**Покажите ми где смо ми сада.** Pokažite mi gde smo mi sada
Here	**Овде** Ovde
There	**Тамо** Tamo
This way	**Овим путем** Ovim putem
Turn right.	**Скрените десно.** Skrenite desno
Turn left.	**Скрените лево.** Skrenite levo
first (second, third) turn	**прво (друго, треће) скретање** prvo (drugo, treće) skretanje

| to the right | **десно** |
| | desno |

| to the left | **лево** |
| | levo |

| Go straight ahead. | **Идите само право.** |
| | Idite samo pravo |

Signs

WELCOME!	**ДОБРОДОШЛИ!** DOBRODOŠLI!
ENTRANCE	**УЛАЗ** ULAZ
EXIT	**ИЗЛАЗ** IZLAZ

PUSH	**ГУРАЈ** GURAJ
PULL	**ВУЦИ** VUCI
OPEN	**ОТВОРЕНО** OTVORENO
CLOSED	**ЗАТВОРЕНО** ZATVORENO

FOR WOMEN	**ЗА ЖЕНЕ** ZA ŽENE
FOR MEN	**ЗА МУШКАРЦЕ** ZA MUŠKARCE
GENTLEMEN, GENTS (m)	**МУШКАРЦИ** MUŠKARCI
WOMEN (f)	**ЖЕНЕ** ŽENE

DISCOUNTS	**ПРОДАЈА** PRODAJA
SALE	**РАСПРОДАЈА** RASPRODAJA
FREE	**БЕСПЛАТНО** BESPLATNO
NEW!	**НОВО!** NOVO!
ATTENTION!	**ПАЖЊА!** PAŽNJA!

NO VACANCIES	**НЕМА СЛОБОДНИХ МЕСТА** NEMA SLOBODNIH MESTA
RESERVED	**РЕЗЕРВИСАНО** REZERVISANO
ADMINISTRATION	**АДМИНИСТРАЦИЈА** ADMINISTRACIJA
STAFF ONLY	**САМО ЗА ЗАПОСЛЕНЕ** SAMO ZA ZAPOSLENE

BEWARE OF THE DOG! **ПАС УЈЕДА!**
PAS UJEDA!

NO SMOKING! **ЗАБРАЊЕНО ПУШЕЊЕ!**
ZABRANJENO PUŠENJE!

DO NOT TOUCH! **НЕ ПИПАЈ!**
NE PIPAJ!

DANGEROUS **ОПАСНО**
OPASNO

DANGER **ОПАСНОСТ**
OPASNOST

HIGH VOLTAGE **ВИСОК НАПОН**
VISOK NAPON

NO SWIMMING! **ЗАБРАЊЕНО ПЛИВАЊЕ!**
ZABRANJENO PLIVANJE!

OUT OF ORDER **НЕ РАДИ**
NE RADI

FLAMMABLE **ЗАПАЉИВО**
ZAPALJIVO

FORBIDDEN **ЗАБРАЊЕНО**
ZABRANJENO

NO TRESPASSING! **ЗАБРАЊЕН ПРОЛАЗ!**
ZABRANJEN PROLAZ!

WET PAINT **СВЕЖЕ ОКРЕЧЕНО**
SVEŽE OKREČENO

CLOSED FOR RENOVATIONS **ЗАТВОРЕНО ЗБОГ РЕНОВИРАЊА**
ZATVORENO ZBOG RENOVIRANJA

WORKS AHEAD **РАДОВИ НА ПУТУ**
RADOVI NA PUTU

DETOUR **ОБИЛАЗАК**
OBILAZAK

Transportation. General phrases

plane	**авион** avion
train	**воз** voz
bus	**аутобус** autobus
ferry	**трајект** trajekt
taxi	**такси** taksi
car	**ауто** auto
schedule	**ред вожње** red vožnje
Where can I see the schedule?	**Где могу да видим ред вожње?** Gde mogu da vidim red vožnje?
workdays (weekdays)	**радни дани** radni dani
weekends	**викенди** vikendi
holidays	**празници** praznici
DEPARTURE	**ОДЛАЗАК** ODLAZAK
ARRIVAL	**ДОЛАЗАК** DOLAZAK
DELAYED	**КАСНИ** KASNI
CANCELLED	**ОТКАЗАН** OTKAZAN
next (train, etc.)	**следећи** sledeći
first	**први** prvi
last	**последњи** poslednji
When is the next ...?	**Када је следећи ...?** Kada je sledeći ...?
When is the first ...?	**Када је први ...?** Kada je prvi ...?

When is the last …?

Када је последњи …?
Kada je poslednji …?

transfer (change of trains, etc.)

пресе辩ање
presedanje

to make a transfer

имати пресе辩ање
imati presedanje

Do I need to make a transfer?

Треба ли да преседам?
Treba li da presedam?

Buying tickets

Where can I buy tickets?	**Где могу да купим карте?** Gde mogu da kupim karte?
ticket	**карта** karta
to buy a ticket	**купити карту** kupiti kartu
ticket price	**цена карте** cena karte

Where to?	**Куда?** Kuda?
To what station?	**До које станице?** Do koje stanice?
I need ...	**Треба ми ...** Treba mi ...
one ticket	**једна карта** jedna karta
two tickets	**две карте** dve karte
three tickets	**три карте** tri karte

one-way	**у једном правцу** u jednom pravcu
round-trip	**повратна** povratna
first class	**прва класа** prva klasa
second class	**друга класа** druga klasa

today	**данас** danas
tomorrow	**сутра** sutra
the day after tomorrow	**прекосутра** prekosutra
in the morning	**ујутру** ujutru
in the afternoon	**после подне** posle podne
in the evening	**увече** uveče

aisle seat	**седиште до пролаза** sedište do prolaza
window seat	**седиште поред прозора** sedište pored prozora
How much?	**Колико?** Koliko?
Can I pay by credit card?	**Могу ли да платим кредитном картицом?** Mogu li da platim kreditnom karticom?

Bus

bus	**Аутобус** Autobus
intercity bus	**међуградски аутобус** međugradski autobus
bus stop	**аутобуска станица** autobuska stanica
Where's the nearest bus stop?	**Где је најближа аутобуска станица?** Gde je najbliža autobuska stanica?
number (bus ~, etc.)	**број** broj
Which bus do I take to get to …?	**Којим аутобусом стижем до …?** Kojim autobusom stižem do …?
Does this bus go to …?	**Да ли овај аутобус иде до …?** Da li ovaj autobus ide do …?
How frequent are the buses?	**Колико често иду аутобуси?** Koliko često idu autobusi?
every 15 minutes	**сваких 15 минута** svakih 15 minuta
every half hour	**сваких пола сата** svakih pola sata
every hour	**сваки сат** svaki sat
several times a day	**неколико пута дневно** nekoliko puta dnevno
… times a day	**… пута дневно** … puta dnevno
schedule	**ред вожње** red vožnje
Where can I see the schedule?	**Где могу да видим ред вожње?** Gde mogu da vidim red vožnje?
When is the next bus?	**Када је следећи аутобус?** Kada je sledeći autobus?
When is the first bus?	**Када је први аутобус?** Kada je prvi autobus?
When is the last bus?	**Када је последњи аутобус?** Kada je poslednji autobus?
stop	**станица** stanica
next stop	**следећа станица** sledeća stanica

last stop (terminus)

последња станица
poslednja stanica

Stop here, please.

Станите овде, молим вас.
Stanite ovde, molim vas

Excuse me, this is my stop.

Извините, ово је моја станица.
Izvinite, ovo je moja stanica

Train

train	воз
	voz
suburban train	приградски воз
	prigradski voz
long-distance train	међуградски воз
	međugradski voz
train station	железничка станица
	železnička stanica
Excuse me, where is the exit to the platform?	Извините, где је излаз до перона?
	Izvinite, gde je izlaz do perona?

Does this train go to ...?	Да ли овај воз иде до ...?
	Da li ovaj voz ide do ...?
next train	следећи воз
	sledeći voz
When is the next train?	Када полази следећи воз?
	Kada polazi sledeći voz?
Where can I see the schedule?	Где могу да видим ред вожње?
	Gde mogu da vidim red vožnje?
From which platform?	Са ког перона?
	Sa kog perona?
When does the train arrive in ...?	Када воз стиже у ...?
	Kada voz stiže u ...?

Please help me.	Молим вас, помозите ми.
	Molim vas, pomozite mi
I'm looking for my seat.	Тражим своје место.
	Tražim svoje mesto
We're looking for our seats.	Ми тражимо своја места.
	Mi tražimo svoja mesta
My seat is taken.	Моје место је заузето.
	Moje mesto je zauzeto
Our seats are taken.	Наша места су заузета.
	Naša mesta su zauzeta

I'm sorry but this is my seat.	Извините, али ово је моје место.
	Izvinite, ali ovo je moje mesto
Is this seat taken?	Да ли је ово место заузето?
	Da li je ovo mesto zauzeto?
May I sit here?	Могу ли овде да седнем?
	Mogu li ovde da sednem?

On the train. Dialogue (No ticket)

Ticket, please.
Карту, молим вас.
Kartu, molim vas

I don't have a ticket.
Немам карту.
Nemam kartu

I lost my ticket.
Изгубио сам карту.
Izgubio sam kartu

I forgot my ticket at home.
Заборавио сам карту код куће.
Zaboravio sam kartu kod kuće

You can buy a ticket from me.
Од мене можете купити карту.
Od mene možete kupiti kartu

You will also have to pay a fine.
Такође ћете морати да платите казну.
Takođe ćete morati da platite kaznu

Okay.
У реду.
U redu

Where are you going?
Где идете?
Gde idete?

I'm going to ...
Идем до ...
Idem do ...

How much? I don't understand.
Колико? Не разумем.
Koliko? Ne razumem

Write it down, please.
Напишите, молим вас.
Napišite, molim vas

Okay. Can I pay with a credit card?
У реду. Да ли могу да платим кредитном картицом?
U redu. Da li mogu da platim kreditnom karticom?

Yes, you can.
Да, можете.
Da, možete

Here's your receipt.
Изволите рачун.
Izvolite račun

Sorry about the fine.
Извините због казне.
Izvinite zbog kazne

That's okay. It was my fault.
У реду је. Моја грешка.
U redu je. Moja greška

Enjoy your trip.
Уживајте у путовању.
Uživajte u putovanju

Taxi

taxi	**такси** taksi
taxi driver	**таксиста** taksista
to catch a taxi	**ухватити такси** uhvatiti taksi
taxi stand	**такси станица** taksi stanica
Where can I get a taxi?	**Где могу да нађем такси?** Gde mogu da nađem taksi?

to call a taxi	**позвати такси** pozvati taksi
I need a taxi.	**Треба ми такси.** Treba mi taksi
Right now.	**Одмах.** Odmah
What is your address (location)?	**Која је ваша адреса?** Koja je vaša adresa?
My address is …	**Моја адреса је …** Moja adresa je …
Your destination?	**Докле идете?** Dokle idete?

Excuse me, …	**Извините …** Izvinite …
Are you available?	**Да ли сте слободни?** Da li ste slobodni?
How much is it to get to …?	**Колико кошта до …?** Koliko košta do …?
Do you know where it is?	**Да ли знате где је?** Da li znate gde je?
Airport, please.	**Аеродром, молим.** Aerodrom, molim
Stop here, please.	**Станите овде, молим вас.** Stanite ovde, molim vas
It's not here.	**Није овде.** Nije ovde
This is the wrong address.	**Ово је погрешна адреса.** Ovo je pogrešna adresa
Turn left.	**скрените лево** skrenite levo
Turn right.	**скрените десно** skrenite desno

How much do I owe you?	**Колико вам дугујем?** Koliko vam dugujem?
I'd like a receipt, please.	**Рачун, молим.** Račun, molim
Keep the change.	**Задржите кусур.** Zadržite kusur

Would you please wait for me?	**Да ли бисте ме сачекали, молим вас?** Da li biste me sačekali, molim vas?
five minutes	**пет минута** pet minuta
ten minutes	**десет минута** deset minuta
fifteen minutes	**петнаест минута** petnaest minuta
twenty minutes	**двадесет минута** dvadeset minuta
half an hour	**пола сата** pola sata

Hotel

Hello.	**Добар дан.** Dobar dan
My name is …	**Ja се зовем …** Ja se zovem …
I have a reservation.	**Имам резервацију.** Imam rezervaciju
I need …	**Треба ми …** Treba mi …
a single room	**једнокреветна соба** jednokrevetna soba
a double room	**двокреветна соба** dvokrevetna soba
How much is that?	**Колико је то?** Koliko je to?
That's a bit expensive.	**То је мало скупо.** To je malo skupo
Do you have anything else?	**Да ли имате неку другу могућност?** Da li imate neku drugu mogućnost?
I'll take it.	**Узећу то.** Uzeću to
I'll pay in cash.	**Платићу готовином.** Platiću gotovinom
I've got a problem.	**Имам проблем.** Imam problem
My … is broken.	**Мoj … је сломљен /Моja… је сломљена/.** Moj … je slomljen /slomljena/
My … is out of order.	**Мoj /Моja/ … не ради.** Moj /Moja/ … ne radi
TV	**телевизор (м)** televizor
air conditioner	**клима уређај (м)** klima uređaj
tap	**славина (ж)** slavina
shower	**туш (м)** tuš
sink	**лавабо (м)** lavabo

safe	**сеф (м)** sef
door lock	**брава (ж)** brava
electrical outlet	**електрична утичница (ж)** električna utičnica
hairdryer	**фен (м)** fen
I don't have …	**Немам …** Nemam …
water	**воде** vode
light	**светла** svetla
electricity	**струје** struje
Can you give me …?	**Можете ли ми дати …?** Možete li mi dati …?
a towel	**пешкир** peškir
a blanket	**ћебе** ćebe
slippers	**папуче** papuče
a robe	**баде-мантил** bade-mantil
shampoo	**мало шампона** malo šampona
soap	**мало сапуна** malo sapuna
I'd like to change rooms.	**Хоћу да заменим собу.** Hoću da zamenim sobu
I can't find my key.	**Не могу да нађем свој кључ.** Ne mogu da nađem svoj ključ
Could you open my room, please?	**Можете ли ми отворити собу, молим вас?** Možete li mi otvoriti sobu, molim vas?
Who's there?	**Ко је тамо?** Ko je tamo?
Come in!	**Уђите!** Uđite!
Just a minute!	**Само тренутак!** Samo trenutak!
Not right now, please.	**Не сада, молим вас.** Ne sada, molim vas
Come to my room, please.	**Дођите у моју собу, молим вас.** Dođite u moju sobu, molim vas

I'd like to order food service.	**Хтео бих да поручим храну.** Hteo bih da poručim hranu
My room number is ...	**Број моје собе је ...** Broj moje sobe je ...

I'm leaving ...	**Одлазим ...** Odlazim ...
We're leaving ...	**Ми одлазимо ...** Mi odlazimo ...
right now	**одмах** odmah
this afternoon	**овог поподнева** ovog popodneva
tonight	**вечерас** večeras
tomorrow	**сутра** sutra
tomorrow morning	**сутра ујутру** sutra ujutru
tomorrow evening	**сутра увече** sutra uveče
the day after tomorrow	**прекосутра** prekosutra

I'd like to pay.	**Хтео бих да платим.** Hteo bih da platim
Everything was wonderful.	**Све је било дивно.** Sve je bilo divno
Where can I get a taxi?	**Где могу да нађем такси?** Gde mogu da nađem taksi?
Would you call a taxi for me, please?	**Да ли бисте ми позвали такси, молим вас?** Da li biste mi pozvali taksi, molim vas?

KAKO STE

How ARE you.

DOBRA

Good.

Restaurant

Can I look at the menu, please?	**Могу ли да погледам мени, молим вас?** Mogu li da pogledam meni, molim vas?
Table for one.	**Сто за једног.** Sto za jednog
There are two (three, four) of us.	**Има нас двоје (троје, четворо).** Ima nas dvoje (troje, četvoro)
Smoking	**За пушаче** Za pušače
No smoking	**За непушаче** Za nepušače
Excuse me! (addressing a waiter)	**Конобар!** Konobar!
menu	**мени** meni
wine list	**винска карта** vinska karta
The menu, please.	**Мени, молим вас.** Meni, molim vas
Are you ready to order?	**Да ли сте спремни да наручите?** Da li ste spremni da naručite?
What will you have?	**Шта бисте хтели?** Šta biste hteli?
I'll have ...	**Ја ћу ...** Ja ću ...
I'm a vegetarian.	**Ја сам вегетеријанац /вегетаријанка/.** Ja sam vegeterijanac /vegetarijanka/
meat	**месо** meso
fish	**рибу** ribu
vegetables	**поврће** povrće
Do you have vegetarian dishes?	**Имате ли вегетеријанска јела?** Imate li vegeterijanska jela?
I don't eat pork.	**Не једем свињетину.** Ne jedem svinjetinu

he/ doesn't eat meat.	**Он /Она/ не једе месо.** On /Ona/ ne jede meso
I am allergic to …	**Алергичан /Алергична/ сам на …** Alergičan /Alergična/ sam na …

Would you please bring me …	**Да ли бисте ми,** **молим вас, донели …** Da li biste mi, molim vas, doneli …
salt | pepper | sugar	**со | бибер | шећер** so | biber | šećer
coffee | tea | dessert	**кафу | чај | десерт** kafu | čaj | dezert
water | sparkling | plain	**воду | газирану | негазирану** vodu | gaziranu | negaziranu
a spoon | fork | knife	**кашику | виљушку | нож** kašiku | viljušku | nož
a plate | napkin	**тањир | салвету** tanjir | salvetu

Enjoy your meal!	**Пријатно!** Prijatno!
One more, please.	**Још једно, молим.** Još jedno, molim
It was very delicious.	**Било је изврсно.** Bilo je izvrsno

check | change | tip	**рачун | кусур | бакшиш** račun | kusur | bakšiš
Check, please. (Could I have the check, please?)	**Рачун, молим.** Račun, molim
Can I pay by credit card?	**Могу ли да платим** **кредитном картицом?** Mogu li da platim kreditnom karticom?
I'm sorry, there's a mistake here.	**Извините, овде је грешка.** Izvinite, ovde je greška

Shopping

Can I help you?	**Могу ли да вам помогнем?** Mogu li da vam pomognem?
Do you have ...?	**Имате ли ...?** Imate li ...?
I'm looking for ...	**Тражим ...** Tražim ...
I need ...	**Треба ми ...** Treba mi ...

I'm just looking.	**Само гледам.** Samo gledam
We're just looking.	**Само гледамо.** Samo gledamo
I'll come back later.	**Вратићу се касније.** Vratiću se kasnije
We'll come back later.	**Вратићемо се касније.** Vratićemo se kasnije
discounts	sale	**попусти	распродаја** popusti	rasprodaja

Would you please show me ...	**Да ли бисте ми, молим вас, показали ...** Da li biste mi, molim vas, pokazali ...
Would you please give me ...	**Да ли бисте ми, молим вас, дали ...** Da li biste mi, molim vas, dali ...
Can I try it on?	**Могу ли да пробам?** Mogu li da probam?
Excuse me, where's the fitting room?	**Извините, где је кабина за пресвлачење?** Izvinite, gde je kabina za presvlačenje?
Which color would you like?	**Коју боју бисте хтели?** Koju boju biste hteli?
size	length	**величина	дужина** veličina	dužina
How does it fit?	**Како ми стоји?** Kako mi stoji?

How much is it?	**Колико кошта?** Koliko košta?
That's too expensive.	**То је прескупо.** To je preskupo

I'll take it.

Узећу то.
Uzeću to

Excuse me, where do I pay?

Извините, где се плаћа?
Izvinite, gde se plaća?

Will you pay in cash or credit card?

Плаћате ли готовином или кредитном картицом?
Plaćate li gotovinom ili kreditnom karticom?

In cash | with credit card

Готовином | кредитном картицом
Gotovinom | kreditnom karticom

Do you want the receipt?

Желите ли рачун?
Želite li račun?

Yes, please.

Да, молим.
Da, molim

No, it's OK.

Не, у реду је.
Ne, u redu je

Thank you. Have a nice day!

Хвала. Пријатно!
Hvala. Prijatno!

In town

Excuse me, please.	**Извините, молим вас …** Izvinite, molim vas …
I'm looking for …	**Тражим …** Tražim …

the subway	**метро** metro
my hotel	**свој хотел** svoj hotel
the movie theater	**биоскоп** bioskop
a taxi stand	**такси станицу** taksi stanicu

an ATM	**банкомат** bankomat
a foreign exchange office	**мењачницу** menjačnicu
an internet café	**интернет кафе** internet kafe
… street	**улицу …** ulicu …
this place	**ово место** ovo mesto

Do you know where … is?	**Знате ли где је …?** Znate li gde je …?
Which street is this?	**Која је ово улица?** Koja je ovo ulica?

Show me where we are right now.	**Покажите ми где смо ми сада.** Pokažite mi gde smo mi sada
Can I get there on foot?	**Могу ли до тамо пешке?** Mogu li do tamo peške?
Do you have a map of the city?	**Имате ли мапу града?** Imate li mapu grada?

How much is a ticket to get in?	**Колико кошта улазница?** Koliko košta ulaznica?
Can I take pictures here?	**Могу ли овде да се сликам?** Mogu li ovde da se slikam?
Are you open?	**Да ли радите?** Da li radite?

| When do you open? | **Када отварате?** |
| | Kada otvarate? |

| When do you close? | **Када затварате?** |
| | Kada zatvarate? |

Money

money	**новац** novac
cash	**готовина** gotovina
paper money	**папирни новац** papirni novac
loose change	**кусур, ситниш** kusur, sitniš
check | change | tip	**рачун | кусур | бакшиш** račun | kusur | bakšiš
credit card	**кредитна картица** kreditna kartica
wallet	**новчаник** novčanik
to buy	**купити** kupiti
to pay	**платити** platiti
fine	**казна** kazna
free	**бесплатно** besplatno
Where can I buy ...?	**Где могу да купим ...?** Gde mogu da kupim ...?
Is the bank open now?	**Да ли је банка отворена сада?** Da li je banka otvorena sada?
When does it open?	**Када се отвара?** Kada se otvara?
When does it close?	**Када се затвара?** Kada se zatvara?
How much?	**Колико?** Koliko?
How much is this?	**Колико ово кошта?** Koliko ovo košta?
That's too expensive.	**То је прескупо.** To je preskupo
Excuse me, where do I pay?	**Извините, где се плаћа?** Izvinite, gde se plaća?
Check, please.	**Рачун, молим.** Račun, molim

Can I pay by credit card?	**Могу ли да платим кредитном картицом?** Mogu li da platim kreditnom karticom?
Is there an ATM here?	**Да ли овде негде има банкомат?** Da li ovde negde ima bankomat?
I'm looking for an ATM.	**Тражим банкомат.** Tražim bankomat

I'm looking for a foreign exchange office.	**Тражим мењачницу.** Tražim menjačnicu
I'd like to change …	**Хтео бих да заменим …** Hteo bih da zamenim …
What is the exchange rate?	**Колики је курс?** Koliki je kurs?
Do you need my passport?	**Да ли вам треба мој пасош?** Da li vam treba moj pasoš?

Time

What time is it?	**Колико је сати?** Koliko je sati?
When?	**Када?** Kada?
At what time?	**У колико сати?** U koliko sati?
now | later | after …	**сада | касније | после …** sada | kasnije | posle …
one o'clock	**један сат** jedan sat
one fifteen	**један и петнаест** jedan i petnaest
one thirty	**пола два** pola dva
one forty-five	**петнаест до два** petnaest do dva
one | two | three	**један | два | три** jedan | dva | tri
four | five | six	**четири | пет | шест** četiri | pet | šest
seven | eight | nine	**седам | осам | девет** sedam | osam | devet
ten | eleven | twelve	**десет | једанаест | дванаест** deset | jedanaest | dvanaest
in …	**за …** za …
five minutes	**пет минута** pet minuta
ten minutes	**десет минута** deset minuta
fifteen minutes	**петнаест минута** petnaest minuta
twenty minutes	**двадесет минута** dvadeset minuta
half an hour	**пола сата** pola sata
an hour	**сат времена** sat vremena

in the morning	**ујутру** ujutru
early in the morning	**рано ујутру** rano ujutru
this morning	**овог јутра** ovog jutra
tomorrow morning	**сутра ујутру** sutra ujutru

in the middle of the day	**за време ручка** za vreme ručka
in the afternoon	**после подне** posle podne
in the evening	**увече** uveče
tonight	**вечерас** večeras

at night	**ноћу** noću
yesterday	**јуче** juče
today	**данас** danas
tomorrow	**сутра** sutra
the day after tomorrow	**прекосутра** prekosutra

What day is it today?	**Који је данас дан?** Koji je danas dan?
It's ...	**Данас је ...** Danas je ...
Monday	**Понедељак** Ponedeljak
Tuesday	**Уторак** Utorak
Wednesday	**Среда** Sreda

Thursday	**Четвртак** Četvrtak
Friday	**Петак** Petak
Saturday	**Субота** Subota
Sunday	**Недеља** Nedelja

Greetings. Introductions

Hello.	**Здраво.** Zdravo
Pleased to meet you.	**Драго ми је што смо се упознали.** Drago mi je što smo se upoznali
Me too.	**И мени.** I meni
I'd like you to meet ...	**Хтео бих да упознаш ...** Hteo bih da upoznaš ...
Nice to meet you.	**Драго ми је што смо се упознали.** Drago mi je što smo se upoznali

How are you?	**Како сте?** Kako ste?
My name is ...	**Ја се зовем ...** Ja se zovem ...
His name is ...	**Он се зове ...** On se zove ...
Her name is ...	**Она се зове ...** Ona se zove ...
What's your name?	**Како се ви зовете?** Kako se vi zovete?
What's his name?	**Како се он зове?** Kako se on zove?
What's her name?	**Како се она зове?** Kako se ona zove?

What's your last name?	**Како се презивате?** Kako se prezivate?
You can call me ...	**Можете ме звати ...** Možete me zvati ...
Where are you from?	**Одакле сте?** Odakle ste?
I'm from ...	**Ја сам из ...** Ja sam iz ...
What do you do for a living?	**Чиме се бавите?** Čime se bavite?

Who is this?	**Ко је ово?** Ko je ovo?
Who is he?	**Ко је он?** Ko je on?
Who is she?	**Ко је она?** Ko je ona?

Who are they?	**Ко су они?** Ko su oni?
This is …	**Ово је …** Ovo je …
my friend (masc.)	**мој пријатељ** moj prijatelj
my friend (fem.)	**моја пријатељица** moja prijateljica
my husband	**мој муж** moj muž
my wife	**моја жена** moja žena
my father	**мој отац** moj otac
my mother	**моја мајка** moja majka
my brother	**мој брат** moj brat
my sister	**моја сестра** moja sestra
my son	**мој син** moj sin
my daughter	**моја ћерка** moja ćerka
This is our son.	**Ово је наш син.** Ovo je naš sin
This is our daughter.	**Ово је наша ћерка.** Ovo je naša ćerka
These are my children.	**Ово су моја деца.** Ovo su moja deca
These are our children.	**Ово су наша деца.** Ovo su naša deca

Farewells

Good bye!	Довиђења! Doviđenja!
Bye! (inform.)	Ћао! Ćao!
See you tomorrow.	Видимо се сутра. Vidimo se sutra
See you soon.	Видимо се ускоро. Vidimo se uskoro
See you at seven.	Видимо се у седам. Vidimo se u sedam
Have fun!	Лепо се проведите! Lepo se provedite!
Talk to you later.	Чујемо се касније. Čujemo se kasnije
Have a nice weekend.	Леп викенд. Lep vikend
Good night.	Лаку ноћ. Laku noć
It's time for me to go.	Време је да кренем. Vreme je da krenem
I have to go.	Морам да кренем. Moram da krenem
I will be right back.	Одмах се враћам. Odmah se vraćam
It's late.	Касно је. Kasno je
I have to get up early.	Морам рано да устанем. Moram rano da ustanem
I'm leaving tomorrow.	Одлазим сутра. Odlazim sutra
We're leaving tomorrow.	Одлазимо сутра. Odlazimo sutra
Have a nice trip!	Лепо се проведите на путу! Lepo se provedite na putu!
It was nice meeting you.	Драго ми је што смо се упознали. Drago mi je što smo se upoznali
It was nice talking to you.	Драго ми је што смо поразговарали. Drago mi je što smo porazgovarali
Thanks for everything.	Хвала на свему. Hvala na svemu

I had a very good time.	**Лепо сам се провео /провела/.** Lepo sam se proveo /provela/
We had a very good time.	**Лепо смо се провели.** Lepo smo se proveli
It was really great.	**Било је супер.** Bilo je super
I'm going to miss you.	**Недостајаћете ми.** Nedostajaćete mi
We're going to miss you.	**Недостајаћете нам.** Nedostajaćete nam

Good luck!	**Срећно!** Srećno!
Say hi to ...	**Поздравите ...** Pozdravite ...

Foreign language

I don't understand.	**Не разумем.** Ne razumem
Write it down, please.	**Можете ли то записати?** Možete li to zapisati?
Do you speak ...?	**Да ли говорите ...?** Da li govorite ...?
I speak a little bit of ...	**Помало говорим ...** Pomalo govorim ...
English	**Енглески** Engleski
Turkish	**Турски** Turski
Arabic	**Арапски** Arapski
French	**Француски** Francuski
German	**Немачки** Nemački
Italian	**Италијански** Italijanski
Spanish	**Шпански** Španski
Portuguese	**Португалски** Portugalski
Chinese	**Кинески** Kineski
Japanese	**Јапански** Japanski
Can you repeat that, please.	**Можете ли то да поновите, молим вас.** Možete li to da ponovite, molim vas
I understand.	**Разумем.** Razumem
I don't understand.	**Не разумем.** Ne razumem
Please speak more slowly.	**Молим вас, говорите спорије.** Molim vas, govorite sporije

Is that correct? (Am I saying it right?)   **Јел' тако?**
Jel' tako?

What is this? (What does this mean?)   **Шта је ово?**
Šta je ovo?

Apologies

Excuse me, please.
Извините, молим вас.
Izvinite, molim vas

I'm sorry.
Извините.
Izvinite

I'm really sorry.
Јако ми је жао.
Jako mi je žao

Sorry, it's my fault.
Извините, ја сам крив.
Izvinite, ja sam kriv

My mistake.
Моја грешка.
Moja greška

May I ...?
Смем ли ...?
Smem li ...?

Do you mind if I ...?
Да ли би вам сметало да ...?
Da li bi vam smetalo da ...?

It's OK.
OK је.
OK je

It's all right.
У реду је.
U redu je

Don't worry about it.
Не брините.
Ne brinite

Agreement

Yes.	**Да.** Da
Yes, sure.	**Да, свакако.** Da, svakako
OK (Good!)	**Добро, важи!** Dobro, važi!
Very well.	**Врло добро.** Vrlo dobro
Certainly!	**Свакако!** Svakako!
I agree.	**Слажем се.** Slažem se
That's correct.	**Тако је.** Tako je
That's right.	**То је тачно.** To je tačno
You're right.	**Ви сте у праву.** Vi ste u pravu
I don't mind.	**Не смета ми.** Ne smeta mi
Absolutely right.	**Потпуно тачно.** Potpuno tačno
It's possible.	**Могуће је.** Moguće je
That's a good idea.	**То је добра идеја.** To je dobra ideja
I can't say no.	**Не могу да одбијем.** Ne mogu da odbijem
I'd be happy to.	**Биће ми задовољство.** Biće mi zadovoljstvo
With pleasure.	**Са задовољством.** Sa zadovoljstvom

Refusal. Expressing doubt

No.	**Не.** Ne
Certainly not.	**Нипошто.** Nipošto
I don't agree.	**Не слажем се.** Ne slažem se
I don't think so.	**Не мислим тако.** Ne mislim tako
It's not true.	**Није истина.** Nije istina
You are wrong.	**Грешите.** Grešite
I think you are wrong.	**Мислим да грешите.** Mislim da grešite
I'm not sure.	**Нисам сигуран /сигурна/.** Nisam siguran /sigurna/
It's impossible.	**Немогуће.** Nemoguće
Nothing of the kind (sort)!	**Нема шансе!** Nema šanse!
The exact opposite.	**Потпуно супротно.** Potpuno suprotno
I'm against it.	**Ја сам против тога.** Ja sam protiv toga
I don't care.	**Баш ме брига.** Baš me briga
I have no idea.	**Немам појма.** Nemam pojma
I doubt it.	**Не мислим тако.** Ne mislim tako
Sorry, I can't.	**Жао ми је, не могу.** Žao mi je, ne mogu
Sorry, I don't want to.	**Жао ми је, не желим.** Žao mi je, ne želim
Thank you, but I don't need this.	**Хвала, али то ми није потребно.** Hvala, ali to mi nije potrebno
It's getting late.	**Већ је касно.** Već je kasno

I have to get up early.

Морам рано да устанем.
Moram rano da ustanem

I don't feel well.

Не осећам се добро.
Ne osećam se dobro

Expressing gratitude

Thank you.
Хвала вам.
Hvala vam

Thank you very much.
Много вам хвала.
Mnogo vam hvala

I really appreciate it.
Заиста то ценим.
Zaista to cenim

I'm really grateful to you.
Заиста сам вам захвалан /захвална/.
Zaista sam vam zahvalan /zahvalna/

We are really grateful to you.
Заиста смо вам захвални.
Zaista smo vam zahvalni

Thank you for your time.
Хвала вам на времену.
Hvala vam na vremenu

Thanks for everything.
Хвала на свему.
Hvala na svemu

Thank you for ...
Хвала вам на ...
Hvala vam na ...

your help
вашој помоћи
vašoj pomoći

a nice time
на лепом проводу
na lepom provodu

a wonderful meal
лепом оброку
lepom obroku

a pleasant evening
лепој вечери
lepoj večeri

a wonderful day
дивном дану
divnom danu

an amazing journey
сјајном путовању
sjajnom putovanju

Don't mention it.
Није то ништа.
Nije to ništa

You are welcome.
Нема на чему.
Nema na čemu

Any time.
У свако доба.
U svako doba

My pleasure.
Било ми је задовољство.
Bilo mi je zadovoljstvo

Forget it.
Заборавите на то.
Zaboravite na to

Don't worry about it.
Не брините за то.
Ne brinite za to

Congratulations. Best wishes

Congratulations!	**Честитам!** Čestitam!
Happy birthday!	**Срећан рођендан!** Srećan rođendan!
Merry Christmas!	**Срећан Божић!** Srećan Božić!
Happy New Year!	**Срећна Нова година!** Srećna Nova godina!

Happy Easter!	**Срећан Ускрс!** Srećan Uskrs!
Happy Hanukkah!	**Срећна Ханука!** Srećna Hanuka!

I'd like to propose a toast.	**Хтео бих да наздравим.** Hteo bih da nazdravim
Cheers!	**Живели!** Živeli!
Let's drink to …!	**Попијмо у име …!** Popijmo u ime …!
To our success!	**За наш успех!** Za naš uspeh!
To your success!	**За ваш успех!** Za vaš uspeh!

Good luck!	**Срећно!** Srećno!
Have a nice day!	**Пријатан дан!** Prijatan dan!
Have a good holiday!	**Уживајте на одмору!** Uživajte na odmoru!
Have a safe journey!	**Срећан пут!** Srećan put!
I hope you get better soon!	**Надам се да ћете се ускоро опоравити!** Nadam se da ćete se uskoro oporaviti!

Socializing

Why are you sad?	**Зашто си тужна?** Zašto si tužna?
Smile! Cheer up!	**Насмеши се! Разведри се!** Nasmeši se! Razvedri se!
Are you free tonight?	**Да ли си слободна вечерас?** Da li si slobodna večeras?
May I offer you a drink?	**Могу ли вам понудити пиће?** Mogu li vam ponuditi piće?
Would you like to dance?	**Да ли сте за плес?** Da li ste za ples?
Let's go to the movies.	**Хајдемо у биоскоп.** Hajdemo u bioskop
May I invite you to ...?	**Могу ли вас позвати у ...?** Mogu li vas pozvati u ...?
a restaurant	**ресторан** restoran
the movies	**биоскоп** bioskop
the theater	**позориште** pozorište
go for a walk	**у шетњу** u šetnju
At what time?	**У колико сати?** U koliko sati?
tonight	**вечерас** večeras
at six	**у шест** u šest
at seven	**у седам** u sedam
at eight	**у осам** u osam
at nine	**у девет** u devet
Do you like it here?	**Да ли ти се допада овде?** Da li ti se dopada ovde?
Are you here with someone?	**Да ли си овде са неким?** Da li si ovde sa nekim?
I'm with my friend.	**Са пријатељем /пријатељицом/.** Sa prijateljem /prijateljicom/

I'm with my friends.	**Са пријатељима.** Sa prijateljima
No, I'm alone.	**Не, сâм сам. /Не, сама сам/.** Ne, sâm sam. /Ne, sama sam/

Do you have a boyfriend?	**Да ли имаш дечка?** Da li imaš dečka?
I have a boyfriend.	**Имам дечка.** Imam dečka
Do you have a girlfriend?	**Да ли имаш девојку?** Da li imaš devojku?
I have a girlfriend.	**Имам девојку.** Imam devojku

Can I see you again?	**Могу ли опет да те видим?** Mogu li opet da te vidim?
Can I call you?	**Могу ли да те позовем?** Mogu li da te pozovem?
Call me. (Give me a call.)	**Позови ме.** Pozovi me
What's your number?	**Који ти је број телефона?** Koji ti je broj telefona?
I miss you.	**Недостајеш ми.** Nedostaješ mi

You have a beautiful name.	**Имате лепо име.** Imate lepo ime
I love you.	**Волим те.** Volim te
Will you marry me?	**Удај се за мене.** Udaj se za mene
You're kidding!	**Шалите се!** Šalite se!
I'm just kidding.	**Само се шалим.** Samo se šalim

Are you serious?	**Да ли сте озбиљни?** Da li ste ozbiljni?
I'm serious.	**Озбиљан сам.** Ozbiljan sam
Really?!	**Стварно?!** Stvarno?!
It's unbelievable!	**То је невероватно!** To je neverovatno!
I don't believe you.	**Не верујем вам.** Ne verujem vam

I can't.	**Не могу.** Ne mogu
I don't know.	**Не знам.** Ne znam

I don't understand you.

Не разумем те.
Ne razumem te

Please go away.

Молим вас, одлазите.
Molim vas, odlazite

Leave me alone!

Оставите ме на миру!
Ostavite me na miru!

I can't stand him.

Не могу да га поднесем.
Ne mogu da ga podnesem

You are disgusting!

Одвратни сте!
Odvratni ste!

I'll call the police!

Зваћу полицију!
Zvaću policiju!

Sharing impressions. Emotions

I like it.	**Свиђа ми се то.** Sviđa mi se to
Very nice.	**Баш лепо.** Baš lepo
That's great!	**То је супер!** To je super!
It's not bad.	**Није лоше.** Nije loše
I don't like it.	**Не свиђа ми се.** Ne sviđa mi se
It's not good.	**Није добро.** Nije dobro
It's bad.	**Лоше је.** Loše je
It's very bad.	**Много је лоше.** Mnogo je loše
It's disgusting.	**Грозно је.** Grozno je
I'm happy.	**Срећан /Срећна/ сам.** Srećan /Srećna/ sam
I'm content.	**Задовољан /Задовољна/ сам.** Zadovoljan /Zadovoljna/ sam
I'm in love.	**Заљубљен /Заљубљена/ сам.** Zaljubljen /Zaljubljena/ sam
I'm calm.	**Миран /Мирна/ сам.** Miran /Mirna/ sam
I'm bored.	**Досадно ми је.** Dosadno mi je
I'm tired.	**Уморан /Уморна/ сам.** Umoran /Umorna/ sam
I'm sad.	**Тужан /Тужна/ сам.** Tužan /Tužna/ sam
I'm frightened.	**Уплашен /Уплашена/ сам.** Uplašen /Uplašena/ sam
I'm angry.	**Љут /Љута/ сам.** Ljut /Ljuta/ sam
I'm worried.	**Забринут /Забринута/ сам.** Zabrinut /Zabrinuta/ sam
I'm nervous.	**Нервозан /Нервозна/ сам.** Nervozan /Nervozna/ sam

I'm jealous. (envious)

Љубоморан /Љубоморна/ сам.
Ljubomoran /Ljubomorna/ sam

I'm surprised.

Изненађен /Изненађена/ сам.
Iznenađen /Iznenađena/ sam

I'm perplexed.

Збуњен /Збуњена/ сам.
Zbunjen /Zbunjena/ sam

Problems. Accidents

I've got a problem.	**Имам проблем.** Imam problem
We've got a problem.	**Имамо проблем.** Imamo problem
I'm lost.	**Изгубио /Изгубила/ сам се.** Izgubio /Izgubila/ sam se
I missed the last bus (train).	**Пропустио /пропустила/ сам последњи аутобус (воз).** Propustio /propustila/ sam poslednji autobus (voz)
I don't have any money left.	**Немам више новца.** Nemam više novca
I've lost my ...	**Изгубио /Изгубила/ сам ...** Izgubio /Izgubila/ sam ...
Someone stole my ...	**Неко ми је украо ...** Neko mi je ukrao ...
passport	**пасош** pasoš
wallet	**новчаник** novčanik
papers	**папире** papire
ticket	**карту** kartu
money	**новац** novac
handbag	**ташну** tašnu
camera	**фото-апарат** foto-aparat
laptop	**лаптоп** laptop
tablet computer	**таблет рачунар** tablet računar
mobile phone	**мобилни телефон** mobilni telefon
Help me!	**Помозите ми!** Pomozite mi!
What's happened?	**Шта се десило?** Šta se desilo?

fire	**пожар** požar
shooting	**пуцњава** pucnjava
murder	**убиство** ubistvo
explosion	**експлозија** eksplozija
fight	**туча** tuča

Call the police!	**Позовите полицију!** Pozovite policiju!
Please hurry up!	**Молим вас, пожурите!** Molim vas, požurite!
I'm looking for the police station.	**Тражим полицијску станицу.** Tražim policijsku stanicu
I need to make a call.	**Морам да телефонирам.** Moram da telefoniram
May I use your phone?	**Могу ли да се послужим вашим телефоном?** Mogu li da se poslužim vašim telefonom?

I've been …	**Неко ме је …** Neko me je …
mugged	**покрао** pokrao
robbed	**опљачкао** opljačkao
raped	**силовао** silovao
attacked (beaten up)	**напао** napao

Are you all right?	**Да ли сте добро?** Da li ste dobro?
Did you see who it was?	**Да ли сте видели ко је то био?** Da li ste videli ko je to bio?
Would you be able to recognize the person?	**Да ли бисте могли да препознате ту особу?** Da li biste mogli da prepoznate tu osobu?
Are you sure?	**Да ли сте сигурни?** Da li ste sigurni?

Please calm down.	**Молим вас, смирите се.** Molim vas, smirite se
Take it easy!	**Само полако!** Samo polako!
Don't worry!	**Не брините!** Ne brinite!

Everything will be fine.	**Све ће бити у реду.** Sve će biti u redu
Everything's all right.	**Све је у реду.** Sve je u redu

Come here, please.	**Дођите, молим вас.** Dođite, molim vas
I have some questions for you.	**Имам питања за вас.** Imam pitanja za vas
Wait a moment, please.	**Сачекајте, молим вас.** Sačekajte, molim vas
Do you have any I.D.?	**Имате ли исправе?** Imate li isprave?
Thanks. You can leave now.	**Хвала. Можете ићи.** Hvala. Možete ići
Hands behind your head!	**Руке иза главе!** Ruke iza glave!
You're under arrest!	**Ухапшени сте!** Uhapšeni ste!

Health problems

Please help me.	**Молим вас, помозите ми.** Molim vas, pomozite mi
I don't feel well.	**Не осећам се добро.** Ne osećam se dobro
My husband doesn't feel well.	**Мој муж се не осећа добро.** Moj muž se ne oseća dobro
My son ...	**Мој син ...** Moj sin ...
My father ...	**Мој отац ...** Moj otac ...
My wife doesn't feel well.	**Моја жена се не осећа добро.** Moja žena se ne oseća dobro
My daughter ...	**Моја ћерка ...** Moja ćerka ...
My mother ...	**Моја мајка ...** Moja majka ...
I've got a ...	**Боли ме ...** Boli me ...
headache	**глава** glava
sore throat	**грло** grlo
stomach ache	**стомак** stomak
toothache	**зуб** zub
I feel dizzy.	**Врти ми се у глави.** Vrti mi se u glavi
He has a fever.	**Он има температуру.** On ima temperaturu
She has a fever.	**Она има температуру.** Ona ima temperaturu
I can't breathe.	**Не могу да дишем.** Ne mogu da dišem
I'm short of breath.	**Не могу да удахнем.** Ne mogu da udahnem
I am asthmatic.	**Ја сам асматичар /асматичарка/.** Ja sam asmatičar /asmatičarka/
I am diabetic.	**Ја сам дијабетичар /дијабетичарка/.** Ja sam dijabetičar /dijabetičarka/

I can't sleep.	**Не могу да спавам.** Ne mogu da spavam
food poisoning	**тровање храном** trovanje hranom

It hurts here.	**Овде ме боли.** Ovde me boli
Help me!	**Помозите ми!** Pomozite mi!
I am here!	**Овде сам!** Ovde sam!
We are here!	**Овде смо!** Ovde smo!
Get me out of here!	**Вадите ме одавде!** Vadite me odavde!
I need a doctor.	**Потребан ми је лекар.** Potreban mi je lekar
I can't move.	**Не могу да се померим.** Ne mogu da se pomerim
I can't move my legs.	**Не могу да померам ноге.** Ne mogu da pomeram noge

I have a wound.	**Имам рану.** Imam ranu
Is it serious?	**Да ли је озбиљно?** Da li je ozbiljno?
My documents are in my pocket.	**Документа су ми у џепу.** Dokumenta su mi u džepu
Calm down!	**Смирите се!** Smirite se!
May I use your phone?	**Могу ли да се послужим вашим телефоном?** Mogu li da se poslužim vašim telefonom?

Call an ambulance!	**Позовите хитну помоћ!** Pozovite hitnu pomoć!
It's urgent!	**Хитно је!** Hitno je!
It's an emergency!	**Хитан случај!** Hitan slučaj!
Please hurry up!	**Молим вас, пожурите!** Molim vas, požurite!
Would you please call a doctor?	**Молим вас, зовите доктора?** Molim vas, zovite doktora?
Where is the hospital?	**Где је болница?** Gde je bolnica?

How are you feeling?	**Како се осећате?** Kako se osećate?
Are you all right?	**Да ли сте добро?** Da li ste dobro?

What's happened?

Шта се десило?
Šta se desilo?

I feel better now.

Сада се осећам боље.
Sada se osećam bolje

It's OK.

OK je.
OK je

It's all right.

У реду је.
U redu je

At the pharmacy

pharmacy (drugstore)	**апотека** apoteka
24-hour pharmacy	**дежурна апотека** dežurna apoteka
Where is the closest pharmacy?	**Где је најближа апотека?** Gde je najbliža apoteka?

Is it open now?	**Да ли је отворена сада?** Da li je otvorena sada?
At what time does it open?	**Када се отвара?** Kada se otvara?
At what time does it close?	**Када се затвара?** Kada se zatvara?

Is it far?	**Да ли је далеко?** Da li je daleko?
Can I get there on foot?	**Могу ли до тамо пешке?** Mogu li do tamo peške?
Can you show me on the map?	**Можете ли да ми покажете на мапи?** Možete li da mi pokažete na mapi?

Please give me something for ...	**Молим вас, дајте ми нешто за ...** Molim vas, dajte mi nešto za ...
a headache	**главобољу** glavobolju
a cough	**кашаљ** kašalj
a cold	**прехладу** prehladu
the flu	**грип** grip

a fever	**температуру** temperaturu
a stomach ache	**стомачне тегобе** stomačne tegobe
nausea	**мучнину** mučninu
diarrhea	**дијареју** dijareju
constipation	**констипацију** konstipaciju
pain in the back	**болове у леђима** bolove u leđima

chest pain	**болове у грудима** bolove u grudima
side stitch	**бол у боку** bol u boku
abdominal pain	**бол у стомаку** bol u stomaku

pill	**пилула** pilula
ointment, cream	**маст, крема** mast, krema
syrup	**сируп** sirup
spray	**спреј** sprej
drops	**капи** kapi

You need to go to the hospital.	**Морате у болницу.** Morate u bolnicu
health insurance	**здравствено осигурање** zdravstveno osiguranje
prescription	**рецепт** recept
insect repellant	**нешто против инсеката** nešto protiv insekata
Band Aid	**фластер** flaster

The bare minimum

Excuse me, ...	**Извините, ...** Izvinite, ...
Hello.	**Добар дан.** Dobar dan
Thank you.	**Хвала вам.** Hvala vam
Good bye.	**Довиђења.** Doviđenja
Yes.	**Да.** Da
No.	**Не.** Ne
I don't know.	**Не знам.** Ne znam
Where? | Where to? | When?	**Где? | Куда? | Када?** Gde? | Kuda? | Kada?
I need ...	**Треба ми ...** Treba mi ...
I want ...	**Хоћу ...** Hoću ...
Do you have ...?	**Имате ли ...?** Imate li ...?
Is there a ... here?	**Да ли овде постоји ...?** Da li ovde postoji ...?
May I ...?	**Смем ли ...?** Smem li ...?
..., please (polite request)	**молим** molim
I'm looking for ...	**Тражим ...** Tražim ...
restroom	**тоалет** toalet
ATM	**банкомат** bankomat
pharmacy (drugstore)	**апотеку** apoteku
hospital	**болницу** bolnicu
police station	**полицијску станицу** policijsku stanicu
subway	**метро** metro

taxi	**такси** taksi
train station	**железничку станицу** železničku stanicu

My name is …	**Ja се зовем …** Ja se zovem …
What's your name?	**Како се ви зовете?** Kako se vi zovete?
Could you please help me?	**Да ли бисте, молим вас, могли да ми помогнете?** Da li biste, molim vas, mogli da mi pomognete?
I've got a problem.	**Имам проблем.** Imam problem
I don't feel well.	**Не осећам се добро.** Ne osećam se dobro
Call an ambulance!	**Позовите хитну помоћ!** Pozovite hitnu pomoć!
May I make a call?	**Смем ли да телефонирам?** Smem li da telefoniram?

I'm sorry.	**Извините …** Izvinite …
You're welcome.	**Нема на чему.** Nema na čemu

I, me	**ja, мене** ja, mene
you (inform.)	**ти** ti
he	**он** on
she	**она** ona
they (masc.)	**они** oni
they (fem.)	**оне** one
we	**ми** mi
you (pl)	**ви** vi
you (sg, form.)	**ви** vi

ENTRANCE	**УЛАЗ** ULAZ
EXIT	**ИЗЛАЗ** IZLAZ
OUT OF ORDER	**НЕ РАДИ** NE RADI

CLOSED	**ЗАТВОРЕНО** ZATVORENO
OPEN	**ОТВОРЕНО** OTVORENO
FOR WOMEN	**ЗА ЖЕНЕ** ZA ŽENE
FOR MEN	**ЗА МУШКАРЦЕ** ZA MUŠKARCE

MINI DICTIONARY

This section contains 250 useful words required for everyday communication. You will find the names of months and days of the week here. The dictionary also contains topics such as colors, measurements, family, and more

T&P Books Publishing

DICTIONARY CONTENTS

T&P Books Publishing

time	време (c)	vreme
hour	сат (м)	sat
half an hour	пола (ж) сата	pola sata
minute	минут (м)	minut
second	секунд (м)	sekund
today (adv)	данас	danas
tomorrow (adv)	сутра	sutra
yesterday (adv)	јуче	juče
Monday	понедељак (м)	ponedeljak
Tuesday	уторак (м)	utorak
Wednesday	среда (ж)	sreda
Thursday	четвртак (м)	četvrtak
Friday	петак (м)	petak
Saturday	субота (ж)	subota
Sunday	недеља (ж)	nedelja
day	дан (м)	dan
working day	радни дан (м)	radni dan
public holiday	празничан дан (м)	prazničan dan
weekend	викенд (м)	vikend
week	недеља (ж)	nedelja
last week (adv)	прошле недеље	prošle nedelje
next week (adv)	следеће недеље	sledeće nedelje
in the morning	ујутру	ujutru
in the afternoon	поподне	popodne
in the evening	увече	uveče
tonight (this evening)	вечерас	večeras
at night	ноћу	noću
midnight	поноћ (ж)	ponoć
January	јануар (м)	januar
February	фебруар (м)	februar
March	март (м)	mart
April	април (м)	april
May	мај (м)	maj
June	јун (м), јуни (м)	jun, juni
July	јули (м)	juli
August	август (м)	avgust

September	септембар (м)	septembar
October	октобар (м)	oktobar
November	новембар (м)	novembar
December	децембар (м)	decembar

in spring	у пролеће	u proleće
in summer	лети	leti
in fall	у јесен	u jesen
in winter	зими	zimi

month	месец (м)	mesec
season (summer, etc.)	сезона (ж)	sezona
year	година (ж)	godina

2. Numbers. Numerals

0 zero	нула	nula
1 one	један	jedan
2 two	два	dva
3 three	три	tri
4 four	четири	četiri

5 five	пет	pet
6 six	шест	šest
7 seven	седам	sedam
8 eight	осам	osam
9 nine	девет	devet
10 ten	десет	deset

11 eleven	једанаест	jedanaest
12 twelve	дванаест	dvanaest
13 thirteen	тринаест	trinaest
14 fourteen	четрнаест	četrnaest
15 fifteen	петнаест	petnaest

16 sixteen	шеснаест	šesnaest
17 seventeen	седамнаест	sedamnaest
18 eighteen	осамнаест	osamnaest
19 nineteen	деветнаест	devetnaest

20 twenty	двадесет	dvadeset
30 thirty	тридесет	trideset
40 forty	четрдесет	četrdeset
50 fifty	педесет	pedeset

60 sixty	шездесет	šezdeset
70 seventy	седамдесет	sedamdeset
80 eighty	осамдесет	osamdeset
90 ninety	деведесет	devedeset
100 one hundred	сто	sto

200 two hundred	**двеста**	dvesta
300 three hundred	**триста**	trista
400 four hundred	**четиристо**	četiristo
500 five hundred	**петсто**	petsto
600 six hundred	**шестсто**	šeststo
700 seven hundred	**седамсто**	sedamsto
800 eight hundred	**осамсто**	osamsto
900 nine hundred	**деветсто**	devetsto
1000 one thousand	**хиљада**	hiljada
10000 ten thousand	**десет хиљада**	deset hiljada
one hundred thousand	**сто хиљада**	sto hiljada
million	**милион** (м)	milion
billion	**милијарда** (ж)	milijarda

3. Humans. Family

man (adult male)	**мушкарац** (м)	muškarac
young man	**младић** (м)	mladić
woman	**жена** (ж)	žena
girl (young woman)	**девојка** (ж)	devojka
old man	**старац** (м)	starac
old woman	**старица** (ж)	starica
mother	**мајка** (ж)	majka
father	**отац** (м)	otac
son	**син** (м)	sin
daughter	**кћи** (ж)	kći
brother	**брат** (м)	brat
sister	**сестра** (ж)	sestra
parents	**родитељи** (мн)	roditelji
child	**дете** (с)	dete
children	**деца** (с мн)	deca
stepmother	**маћеха** (ж)	maćeha
stepfather	**очух** (м)	očuh
grandmother	**бака** (ж)	baka
grandfather	**деда** (м)	deda
grandson	**унук** (м)	unuk
granddaughter	**унука** (ж)	unuka
grandchildren	**унуци** (мн)	unuci
uncle	**ујак, стриц** (м)	ujak, stric
aunt	**ујна, стрина** (ж)	ujna, strina
nephew	**синовац** (м)	sinovac
niece	**синовица** (ж)	sinovica
wife	**жена** (ж)	žena

husband	муж (м)	muž
married (masc.)	ожењен	oženjen
married (fem.)	удата	udata
widow	удовица (ж)	udovica
widower	удовац (м)	udovac

| name (first name) | име (с) | ime |
| surname (last name) | презиме (с) | prezime |

relative	рођак (м)	rođak
friend (masc.)	пријатељ (м)	prijatelj
friendship	пријатељство (с)	prijateljstvo

partner	партнер (м)	partner
superior (n)	начелник (м)	načelnik
colleague	колега (м)	kolega
neighbors	комшије (мн)	komšije

4. Human body

body	тело (с)	telo
heart	срце (с)	srce
blood	крв (ж)	krv
brain	мозак (м)	mozak

bone	кост (ж)	kost
spine (backbone)	кичма (ж)	kičma
rib	ребро (с)	rebro
lungs	плућа (с мн)	pluća
skin	кожа (ж)	koža

head	глава (ж)	glava
face	лице (с)	lice
nose	нос (м)	nos
forehead	чело (с)	čelo
cheek	образ (м)	obraz

mouth	уста (с мн)	usta
tongue	језик (м)	jezik
tooth	зуб (м)	zub
lips	усне (ж мн)	usne
chin	брада (ж)	brada

ear	ухо (с)	uho
neck	врат (м)	vrat
eye	око (с)	oko
pupil	зеница (ж)	zenica
eyebrow	обрва (ж)	obrva
eyelash	трепавица (ж)	trepavica
hair	коса (ж)	kosa

hairstyle	фризура (ж)	frizura
mustache	брокви (м мн)	brkovi
beard	брада (ж)	brada
to have (a beard, etc.)	носити	nositi
bald (adj)	ћелав	ćelav

hand	шака (ж)	šaka
arm	рука (ж)	ruka
finger	прст (м)	prst
nail	нокат (м)	nokat
palm	длан (ж)	dlan

shoulder	раме (с)	rame
leg	нога (ж)	noga
knee	колено (с)	koleno
heel	пета (ж)	peta
back	леђа (мн)	leđa

5. Clothing. Personal accessories

clothes	одећа (ж)	odeća
coat (overcoat)	капут (м)	kaput
fur coat	бунда (ж)	bunda
jacket (e.g., leather ~)	јакна (ж)	jakna
raincoat (trenchcoat, etc.)	кишни мантил (м)	kišni mantil

shirt (button shirt)	кошуља (ж)	košulja
pants	панталоне (ж мн)	pantalone
suit jacket	сако (м)	sako
suit	одело (с)	odelo

dress (frock)	хаљина (ж)	haljina
skirt	сукња (ж)	suknja
T-shirt	мајица (ж)	majica
bathrobe	баде мантил (м)	bade mantil
pajamas	пиџама (ж)	pidžama
workwear	радно одело (с)	radno odelo

underwear	доње рубље (с)	donje rublje
socks	чарапе (ж мн)	čarape
bra	грудњак (м)	grudnjak
pantyhose	грилонке (ж мн)	grilonke
stockings (thigh highs)	хулахопке (ж мн)	hulahopke
bathing suit	купаћи костим (м)	kupaći kostim

hat	капа (ж)	kapa
footwear	обућа (ж)	obuća
boots (e.g., cowboy ~)	чизме (ж мн)	čizme
heel	потпетица (ж)	potpetica
shoestring	пертла (ж)	pertla

shoe polish	крема (ж) за обућу	krema za obuću
gloves	рукавице (ж мн)	rukavice
mittens	рукавице (ж мн)	rukavice
scarf (muffler)	шал (м)	šal
glasses (eyeglasses)	наочари (м мн)	naočari
umbrella	кишобран (м)	kišobran

tie (necktie)	кравата (ж)	kravata
handkerchief	џепна марамица (ж)	džepna maramica
comb	чешаљ (м)	češalj
hairbrush	четка (ж) за косу	četka za kosu

buckle	копча (ж)	kopča
belt	пас (м)	pas
purse	ташна (ж)	tašna

6. House. Apartment

apartment	стан (м)	stan
room	соба (ж)	soba
bedroom	спаваћа соба (ж)	spavaća soba
dining room	трпезарија (ж)	trpezarija

living room	дневна соба (ж)	dnevna soba
study (home office)	кабинет (м)	kabinet
entry room	предсобље (с)	predsoblje
bathroom (room with a bath or shower)	купатило (с)	kupatilo
half bath	тоалет (м)	toalet

vacuum cleaner	усисивач (м)	usisivač
mop	џогер (м)	džoger
dust cloth	крпа (ж)	krpa
short broom	метла (ж)	metla
dustpan	ђубровник (м)	đubrovnik

furniture	намештај (м)	nameštaj
table	сто (м)	sto
chair	столица (ж)	stolica
armchair	фотеља (ж)	fotelja

mirror	огледало (с)	ogledalo
carpet	тепих (м)	tepih
fireplace	камин (м)	kamin
drapes	завесе (ж мн)	zavese
table lamp	стона лампа (ж)	stona lampa
chandelier	лустер (м)	luster

| kitchen | кухиња (ж) | kuhinja |
| gas stove (range) | плински шпорет (м) | plinski šporet |

| electric stove | електрички шпорет (м) | električki šporet |
| microwave oven | микроталасна рерна (ж) | mikrotalasna rerna |

refrigerator	фрижидер (м)	frižider
freezer	замрзивач (м)	zamrzivač
dishwasher	машина (ж) за прање судова	mašina za pranje sudova
faucet	славина (ж)	slavina

meat grinder	машина (ж) за млевење меса	mašina za mlevenje mesa
juicer	соковник (м)	sokovnik
toaster	тостер (м)	toster
mixer	миксер (м)	mikser

coffee machine	аппарат (м) за кафу	apparat za kafu
kettle	кувало, чајник (м)	kuvalo, čajnik
teapot	чајник (м)	čajnik

TV set	телевизор (м)	televizor
VCR (video recorder)	видео рекордер (м)	video rekorder
iron (e.g., steam ~)	пегла (ж)	pegla
telephone	телефон (м)	telefon

Printed in Great Britain
by Amazon